His Light In My Darkness

CW01498229

Spoken Thiiird

BookLeaf
Publishing

India | USA | UK

Presentation by *BookLeaf Publishing*

Web: www.bookleafpub.com

E-mail: info@bookleafpub.com

ISBN: 9789358317046

First edition 2024

:

'A Guru is like a beautiful street lamp. It cannot make your distance shorter but can lighten your path to make the journey easier.'

- Pujya Gurudevshri Rakeshji *(2013)*

Signed by my Magnanimous Guru in my first book.

Previous Work

Books:

Ideal Idol Idle Series
Part 1: Untitled *(2013)*
Part 2: The wondering mind of a troubled soul
(2014)
Part 3: The Incomparable Extrordinaires *(2015)*
(available on www.thiiirdworld.co.uk)

Diary of a Pilgrim *(2019)*
*(available on Amazon UK &
www.thiiirdworld.co.uk)*

Plays:

'The Life of Jesus Christ' performed in Girnar
& Dharampur, India *(2013)*

'Anaekantvad: A Play on Multidimensional
Truth' performed in Birmingham England
(2017)

'Global Youth production of Patrank
108' performed in London *(2018)*

'You remind me my Lord' performed
in Blackburn *(2023)*

Albums:

Effortless - By Spoken Thiiird & Faith *(2019)*

TOJ - By Spoken Thiiird *(2022)*
(available on
www.soundcloud.com/spokenthiiird/sets/toj)

Podcast:

Thiiird Eye View Podcast
(available on all podcast platforms)

Its that Deep
(available on all podcast platforms)

Available at:

Website: www.thiiirdworld.co.uk
Email: spokenthiiird@gmail.com
Instagram: @spokenthiiird
Twitter: @spokenthiiird
Youtube: @ThiiirdWorld

In Eternal Memory of my lovely Shireen.

My best friend, my sister, my soulmate.

This book is another way to immortalise your legacy and preserve our love. Your beloved daughter Avni will know how special her mother was as she became the light while defeating her darkness.

Thank you for blessing me to be your brother and a mama to our beautiful Avni.
Until we meet again, sis.

From Yours, always and forever.

ACKNOWLEDGEMENT

Thank you to Hridya Manek who sent this challenge to me. When I was looking for inspiration, her message prompted me to write to my heart's content once again.

Thank you to all the challenges and hurdles that have come into my life, which as an artist and poet, fuel my work. They become personal learnings, and an opportunity to further explore the deepest parts of myself.

Thank you to you, the reader. Thank you for being part of this journey and for choosing to pick up this book.

PREFACE

This book is my attempt to express myself and to write as freely as possible. It is unpolished, raw and truthful, forming a bridge from the worst to the best parts of me.

This book starts and ends with three poems which serve as an introduction and conclusion to the book. The rest of the twenty-seven poems are in three sections; my questioning mind, my flawed character and my deep emotions. The poems that are more thought-provoking have a question mark within the title, while the poems that are from an emotional perspective have a colour in their title. The poems that form a reflection of my character are titled with 'Mr.'

Within these poems I mention 'He/Him'. This is when I am speaking about my Guide, my Guru, my God. He has shown me the light within myself. Each poem is a journey from being ignorantly low to His enlightened high.

I pray that you can connect to this book of poetry and it can lead you to finding the light within yourself, even if at times we feel we are at a dead end. I hope this can be a book of hope, this offering can offer comfort, this   devotion can enhance your own.

I bring to you: His Light In My Darkness.

Dedication:

I dedicate this book, as I do my life, to The One so bright He shone a light upon me. He showed me my darkness, and only through His burning love it has begun to dissipate.

The literal meaning of a Guru is: the one who takes His disciples from the darkness of ignorance to the light of knowledge. My Guru does this over and over again. A lifetime of thanks would be too little.

Thank you Pujya Gurudevshri Rakeshji, I bow down to You an infinite number of times.

Contents Page

Chapter 3 - Colourful Hearts

Purposeful Endings

Unusual Beginnings

Guide to the Guide

The way I have lived upon the moment I die
I wish they see me as the guide to The Guide
Nothing I have learnt can be hidden in disguise
Everything I know came from my one true
Guide

People love me, they feel inspired by the words
that I write
Compliment me on being able to shed new light
On ideas and truths that were hidden from their
view
They say I am able to make them see through

A whole new way of perceiving
From dreaming to being
From existing to living
From inhaling to breathing
From thinking to feeling

From the enduring dark to the consuming light
I do this because I only write about my Guide
The way I have lived upon the moment I die
I wish they see me as the guide to The Guide.

Rendezvous

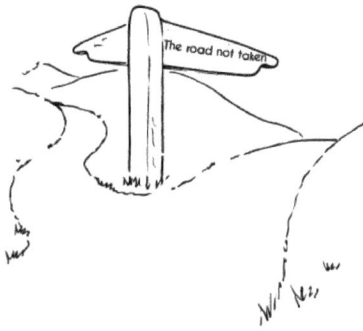

For Him it was a rendezvous
For me it was another day
He saw me in His inner views
I saw Him in my eye's way

He blocked out the path that I was used to
treading
I had no plans to walk towards a new heading
I was young, wild and free with a million roads
to travel
Who was He to judge me, His hands held no
gavel

So what if the gravel underneath my feet was
rough and tough

There will be a junction ahead which leads to
peace and love
This is what is promised to all who have faith in
the world
The hope of happiness is around the corner for
every boy and girl

Just keep swimming said Dory who forgets her
name
One more sea to dive into to wash away the pain
We are heading to the promised land, it's just on
the right
But why are my eyes left distracted by the
brightness of His light?

For Him it was a Rendezvous
For me it was another day
He saw me in His inner views
I saw Him in my eyes' way

He didn't block my path, He showed me another
route
He asked me to examine my past to see if I was
on the right commute
To ask myself if going back and forth would
lead me to moving ahead
How can being stuck in a cycle be a way to
handle life and death?

4

Is the false paradise I have created actually
destitute?
In the Eden I have imagined I must look at every
shoot
The trees which held my beliefs I must see its
deepest root
Is this the reason why my life wasn't bearing
fruit?

Have I got Dory syndrome forgetting why I'm in
pain?
Wilful amnesia to still have hope in the 'one day'
That one wake will be a morning when I'll be in
eternal peace
The dead must rest in it as living feels to be a
constant unease

For Him it was a Rendezvous
For me it was another day
He saw me in His inner views
I saw Him in my eye's way

He knew this Rendezvous would lead me to
heaven's gates
And I would run there on His wings if that be
my fate
But serving Him was my paradise and route to
be free

All I had to do was open my three eyes and finally see.

His Little Light

His little light of mine
I'm going to let it shine
His little light of mine
I'm going to let it shine
His little light of mine
I'm going to let it shine
To free the blind
To free the blind
To free the blind

On Monday He gave me the gift of fun
Treated me like I was His favourite son
Made me laugh, smile and dance to the beat of
His drum
Lost myself in His glory and my heart He had
won

On Tuesday He gave me the gift of doubt
All of a sudden I was confused about
What seeds I have planted and what can sprout
What should stay in my mind and what I can do
without

On Wednesday He gave me the gift of love
Aligned my being to His rays from above
Made me feel light and free like the wings of
doves
The diamond heart is more useful than spades or
clubs

On Thursday He gave me the gift of trust
Let me heal all the parts within that had begun to
rust
Let me clean all my relationships that had begun
to dust
Made me see His way for me is now the only
must

On Friday He gave me the gift of truth
Let me drink His words in from the fountain of
His youth
Inspiring me with His voice which feels velvety
and smooth
He blesses my future by giving me His right to
choose

On Saturday He gave me the gift of peace
Showed me how closing my eyes is the way for
me to see
By increasing my silence it decreases my needs
By letting go of my wants it allows for Him to
lead

On Sunday He gave me the gift of sight
Igniting my inner fire to become burning bright
He freed me from the darkness of the coldest
night
Now all I am is a hand which holds His
everlasting light

His everlasting light

His little light of mine
I'm going to let it shine
To free the blind
To free the blind
To free the blind.

Chapter 1 - Questioning Mind

Why me?

Why does it always rain on me?
Is it because I lied throughout my teens
Told my parents stories of make believe
Their karma for telling me fairy tales to put me
to sleep

But why me?

Why am I still single when my friends lay with
their chosen lover every night?
Why did I decide to be an entrepreneur when I
could have just worked a nine to five?
Why did I become a writer when I could have
been the reader of others' vulnerabilities?

Why do I continue to be a seeker when
traditional beliefs could have fulfilled all my
mental needs?

Why me?

I never look my age because growing a beard
betrays me
My forehead and lips are bigger than average,
sometimes it plagues me
I'm shorter and skinnier than my personality
even though that's what portrays me
My voice is deep and strong, when I speak, they
feel they must debate me

Why am I me?

Is my life a combination of my free choices or is
destiny at play?
Is this God pulling me along or have I already
determined my way
Is it my fate that I would question if fate plays a
role in my past, future and present
Or is it my choice if there is a hellish fire
burning within me or if I can feel the tranquil
seas of heaven

Can He tell me, why am I me?

He once told me life is like chess,
It is your choice which piece to push
But they can only travel to certain squares

He once told me life isn't stress
If you know when to share or shush
And see the others response as fair

He said that iii am
Who iii am
There is only ever going to be one of me

He said my uniqueness is my superpower
Be grateful that you can ask 'Why has God
chosen me?'

Everyone has their role to play
Story to write
Experiences to feel

Everyone has their debt to pay
Their darkness and light
Their Gods to kneel

Whatever life does throw
Whichever way life does flow
Instead of asking why does it rain on me?

Can you detach your mind
Respond with light
So your internal sky remains cloud free?

Say: Thank God
iii am
Me.

Effortless truth?

The truth is
I don't know what truth is
I heard it's exclusive, objective, elusive

Like trying to hold light in your palms
Or using words to cure pain like charms
I heard only a few are as lucky as Ram
To be still like Mahavir through the chaos and
calm

Like Jesus, Moses, Mohammed those Prophets
who profit
From luck, destiny, karma they have gained and
deposit

In lifetimes of surplus
I really don't know much
I just know truth cannot be for me

As it doesn't come easy or for free

We must sit in service or roam around the
churches
Use a magnifying glass closely to Biblical verses
Or spend our whole life looking up to the
universes
To know the last truth lies where the hearse is

Underground dead and buried in a place that is
hidden
The idea we are all going to die can never be
forgiven
So why try and figure out truth which is used to
makes things harder to see
These things are only for the eyes of mystics and
priests

He told me:
Truth is simple
It is attainable
Why am iii making it so difficult?

Truth is open
There are no obstructions,
It is a gateway that is open to everyone.

Effortless success?

I need to be the very best
I need to move mountains before my arms can
rest
I need to believe I have been born with an 'S' on
my chest
As only Superman mentality can conquer
success

I need all the clothes, all the houses and the
multiple cars
I need the earth, the moon and I'll even take
Mars
And even if that doesn't get me far
I need a spaceship so I can claim the stars

I need everything but more importantly
everyone needs to know it's mine!
What's the point of my glow if they can't see me
shine?
So, I'll scratch my name on the surface of the
moon when I land
Make the stars align to form a picture of my
name as planned
A new constellation for everyone to know
That I have a success that the heavens can't let
go

After space, I need to master time so give me
every clock that exits
I'll even have the might to turn Big Ben into Big
Kish
Because then I will be able to make up for my
past mistakes
The present master of time will always know
what the future makes

Call me greedy, call me empty, call me 'Dr
Strange' but this is my truth.
I need everything, otherwise what is there left to
do?

He told me:
Be my Nothing
That's my something,

There is nothing beyond this finding.

Leave your ego,
Don't walk solo,
Just don't ever let go of me.

Faith?

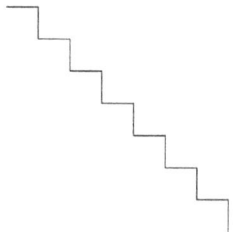

Faith is easy when it matches what you can see
Some would say that's not even faith, that's more
logic and rationality
If I can see the next step on the staircase ahead
of me
I can walk on it securely and effortlessly
Yet what if you can't see the next step, would
you still take the leap?
What if He whispered to you and said:

'My child, have faith in me! Move your feet.'
Faith is putting your heart, mind and actions into
His hands because you realise
That His real eyes can see much further and
clearer than my two opal lies

A rational man has no faith in faith, they find it
irrational
The same man will never ask for the pilots
credentials when flying international
We all operate in faith, my question to you is
where is it placed?
For some it is pages in a book
For others it's in their experience of grace.
Where you leave it, that is your faith.

Peace of mind?

My thoughts are uncontrollable always flying
around and dividing
Just like atoms in C.E.R.N, flying
up
and
down
and colliding

I'm concerned and intrigued
About what path the start of this thought
Will turn to and lead

Will it be a mystery of the future or
contemplation of a past event?
It could trigger a trigger and the wrong turn
could lead me to past regrets
Others may make me boil and steam
Or shiver or scream

Or remind me why
It's so amazing be be alive
Then question if that feeling is marked by the
shadow of pride
All kinds of thoughts linger in my mind

They prevent me from being content
But there is a weird joy to being in resent
I torment myself to what coulda, shoulda,
woulda been
Day dream about the possibilities in which my
life is forever green
I love living in my fantasies where no one can
intervene

Just me and my imagination
Where every idea is worth exploration
Going so deep into them to only find I've just
scratched the surface
And when I resurface from my contemplation I
am frustrated that everyone else only sees the
surface
Feel they lack depth as they are stuck in their
own lives
Yet when I deep it
And see their secret
I envy them, as it's worse to be stuck in your
own mind

I'm just travelling through ideas mentally
As the present moment is the hardest place for
me to be

I am using my mind constantly, it is
uncomfortable
A mental dis-ease, it has become ungovernable.
How do I let it rest, how do I let it be?
Can it ever return to being empty?

Anxiety in silence
Head hurting with all the noise
I've treated my mind to violence
There must be another choice?

Can I ever just be?
Can I just be?
I just be?
I be?
Be?
.

He told me

Peace of mind

Is when you find

A way to let

EVERYTHING

Be.

So you can

Just

Be.

f r e e

It's that deep?

A simple mind is all I need
I keep my feet on the surface
Nothing too deep
Why bring complexity of purpose when you can
choose ease
The simple way of thinking is always the
remedy for peace
Occam's razor in my hand when ideas are
represented to me
Cut away all the parts that make me contemplate
my beliefs

I know the difference between right and wrong,
It's black and white,
Like left and right
And short and long

It's as clear as day and night
And dark and light
And film and song
I know the difference between right and wrong

You live your life so every sense is elated
A Midas touch to pave the way to richness you
have created
Your ears are treated to strings and horns
Your nose only knows the waft of roses no
thorns
Your eyes are hypnotised to see symmetry and
beauty
Your tongue is satiated with gluttony to envy a
foodie

It's not that deep, it's whatever you feel
Only you know what is fake and what is real
Only you know what is best for your senses,
which is you
It's not that deep, it's really simple
uncomplicated truth

He listened to me explain my view
Then asked me a question, which iii ask to you:
Do you want a simple mind or a simple life?
A simple mind is like the bluntest knife.

Higher thinking is the only way to live simply

To inhale deeply is the only way to breathe
freely
Question everything you think until it reaches a
bottomless well
To get there you have to pass through the
shadow of your own hell
But when you see beyond what you think is you
Only then would you have touched truth
Find the deepest inner ocean and dive straight in
to wake from your sleep
I am Your guide, you'll meet Me when you get
that deep.

Life is chess?

I push my pawn, it lands on B4
This was before I knew this was a rookie
mistake
The black pieces respond with a gambit, while I
am wondering when I will get to checkmate?

You see I am playing with the end in mind
The other side is just playing one move at a time
I rush in with my Queen
Hoping it's horsepower will mean
I am the driver of this kingdom

They respond with smaller moves
I am already perturbed
It's like they are using some kind of wisdom

I muster the courage and go for the King
I can see a way for me to win,
In three-moves-time I will have defeated my
enemy

But in my haste I fail to check
If my monarch is safe to rest
Unknowingly my opponent is already ahead of
me

They move this way and that
My plan is scuppered and I am trapped
I am resigned to falling victim to their fate

In my rush to defeat their King
I am the one who didn't win
My foe moves their Queen and I lose to a back
rank checkmate!

He shared the game of chess is for the slow and
steady,
The ones who are ready
To bide their time and not to rush in
With brute force and with one track thinking
But to allow trains of thoughts to enter your
mind
Always thinking what the other side wants
It isn't just you who is on the board

Sometimes taking a step back can lead one
towards
Victory
Defeating the enemy
Out manoeuvring your deadliest nemesis
As the 64 squares
Is a true test
Whether one can play every move without
prejudice
The one with the patience of night and day
Will process a way to carve out their own fate
The grandest of masters know
That you have to take each move within the
overall flow
Chess is like life you have to respond and not to
react
To be able to see the fact that chess is just an act
The more detached you can be, every move can
be more exact
Play as best as you can, as your opponent you do
want to outfox
But remember the pawn, Queen and King go
back in the same box.

Reason enough?

Since we knew
That one plus one is two
It opened up a whole new truth
That the universe can be viewed through

Physics and mathematics
Derivatives and quadratics
Exponentials and geometry
Sequentials and trigonometry

Laplace's demon is omniscient
Newton's apple is sufficient
Einstein's theory is complete
Darwin traced us to beings who compete

For survival as it isn't a given, it's something we
have to fight for

And if it comes to it, my survival is what I have
to die for
This is just the way it is, it's unreasonable for us
to think of us as more
As what matters is the play of matter, colliding
randomly in its own war

We are here to briefly exist, but to no real end
Just to be reasonable and to be straight with life
There is nothing to uncover, nothing to
transcend
As even the mighty cosmos will one day run out
of time

He smirked at my logic
Was dismayed by my conclusion
Asked me: 'If iii was truly scientific
Would iii stop seeking a solution'

If everything was already discovered
And everything was already known
Why do humans still mentally suffer
If all they are is flesh and bone

What if there is a dimension
That mathematics cannot prove
But if given time, space and attention
It will keep you absolutely still and forever
moved

Why don't you experiment within, instead of
being in your head
It's unreasonable to think that you can think up
who is thinking inside
There is yourself to uncover, dark internal
matters to transcend
Through your ignorant darkness you'll see your
true light.

Love my enemy?

Love is precious, I can't give it away so easily
I must give it to those who give ease to me
The special ones who bring peace to me
The ones who bring joy to me, I will give them a
piece of me

The rest of you, the most I can do is to be kind
You are strangers, our life isn't intertwined
My love is for the ones who see me, so it can
never be blind
I must see if you are worthy for me to share my
heart and mind

The ones who have wronged me you are my
enemy
Before you I was so heavenly

I hate that because of you, I created a hell in me
You must pay the highest penalty for breaking
my ecstasy

Love thy enemy? What, why?
They have created pain in me, I'd rather die.
Then to love the ones who have blackened my
sky
I am willing to go blind if it is an eye for an eye

Love thy enemy? What why?
They have created pain in me, I'd rather die.
Then to love the ones who have blackened my
sky
I am willing to go blind if it is an eye for an eye

He looked me in my eyes with tears in His
Showed me the walls iii created had become an
abyss
The hate that iii was feeling was blocking out
my bliss
Love was something to be not something to give

He said the scent of flowers is a consequence of
who they've become
If you are pure, peaceful and powerful love is a
natural outcome
There will be nothing to heal if you have never
had a wound

36

You haven't given anything away you have just
bloomed

He told me to become love and and then you
will see
You won't have to love an enemy because
everyone will just become a reflection of Me
You will see God in everyone like they are all
connected to the above
Then if you become God's child, all that's left is
love.

Chapter 2 - My Characters

Mr Wonderkid

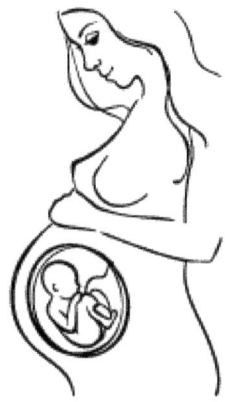

I was supposed to be the G.O.A.T by now
Ruler of the seven seas I should have had my
own boat by now
Gardening money trees I should have had my
own note by now
I was born a wonder kid I was supposed to be
the G.O.A.T by now

There was so much promise about who I would
become
When the number one grandchild would reach
number one
Where light would pour out of me eclipsing the
sun

Where I would fly across the world Cruising
past Top Gun

Gosh, there was so much hype about who I
would be
Pressure makes diamonds but what if it just
crushed me
Paralysed me from moving and achieving all
their dreams
What if the weight of expectation was just too
heavy for me

My school said I was gifted and talented
My parents insisted I was multifaceted
My family put me on a pedestal, some just to see
me topple and fall
Friends remained sceptical, laughing at my tall
dreams because it made them feel small

I was wondrous about the world that's what I
found to be wonderful
Most have straight black and white vision my
eyes bend to be prideful and colourful
Most willingly follow the crowd I found comfort
in being a leader
Most minds have no space for dreamers, creators
and soul seekers

They said I was a wonder kid and they still tried
to box me in
I was breaking down perceptions in the way they
were seeing
But they wanted me to succeed in what they
determined as success
They dismissed me because they could only see
what I materially didn't possess

I was broke to them, they didn't see my
wholeness out of my lack of bank
They see me as undateable, a filthy fella whose
relationships always tank
I wonder the thoughts of my younger sisters and
brothers
Are they shaking their heads at me like Jordy,
thinking why do I bother?
My younger married siblings must be dreaming
about the next generation
That is who I write my stories for, to touch their
hearts with the products of my creation

They must think of me as a failed wonder kid, I
wonder
How?
When their kids, kids will be moved by the fact
that I did wonder
Now!

My clarity and confidence come from my
relationship with Him
He was the first one to see my true potential
He was the one who showed me how to make
myself essential
Without me knowing He was the one who gave
me the pen
His pages express a way to live forever and
never die again
The ink to write a way to freedom
The poetry to inspire all of God's children
He gave me the stage and the vision to be who
iii was meant to be
The wonder kid who went away from societal
norms to fulfil His prophecy
That iii would be the one to spread His name,
glory and life
And show the world the true vision of my
enlightened Guide.

Mr Addict

I need You, all the time,
You are the only thing that comes to my mind
All I see is your shadow looming around me
I'll block out the light to be in your company

When I am with company, I'm dreaming about
when me and you are alone
When I am away from you, my heart seems to
turn to stone
This is the opposite of Medusa syndrome
Because when you gaze into my eyes, I come
back alive, escaping my tombstone

My grave mistake is needing You all the time
You are the only thing in my mind
Your shadow has now entered me
There is no light in your deadly company

He came to me and asked if iii wanted to be free

I said I do but I have an addictive personality
How do I escape from this prison that I have
made
How can I see the light when my eyes are stuck
on the shade

He said no problem and told to me do one thing
Don't leaving anything
Become addicted to Him

From the depths of the dark, my eyes found the
whitest of lights
From the lowliest lows, my eyes saw the might
of His height
And all the bondages that were holding me
down
Effortlessly fell away when iii noticed His
crown
Because when you see that He is the King of
Kings
You simply leave everything
You become addicted to Him.

Mr Restart

I cleaned my room today
I wanted a fresh start
A new beginning,
A new chapter
A brand new chance
A new lease of life
That is not burdened by
Anything that holds me down
I cleaned my room today
But I couldn't wipe off this frown

I got new clothes today
I wanted to feel brand new
New jeans
New jacket
A pair of brand new shoes

A new way of being seen
Looking fresh and looking clean
Tired of feeling incomplete
I got some new clothes today
But self love didn't fit me

I made a promise today
I wanted to feel I can achieve
To be brave
To be strong
To be more than current me
A commitment that I can change
That I can rise from my darkest shame
That tomorrow I will not be the same old me
I made a promise today
But my mind decided to disagree

He came and said that my room has never been
cleaner
Apart from the dirt and mud that iii have left on
my mirror

He came and said that my new outfit made me
look super duper fly
Apart from all the masks iii was wearing inside

He said my promise were noble and written
down immaculately
Apart from them being hollow, worn, something
that iii wouldn't keep

He said if you truly want to restart something
you have to be brutally true
Because one day there will not be a tomorrow
where you can become anew
Commitment needs to be stronger and stickier
than the mightiest glue
And stick it to me, because then iii will bleed, if
you don't stick to your truth.

Mr Failure

Amen
They tell me to brush my shoulders off and try
again
Dear friend
When you've hit rock bottom and reached the
end
To start again, to go back to the beginning
Feels like asking a dead man to go back to living
Preposterous and impossible
My self-doubt is relentless and unstoppable

How can I garner the energy, courage and
strength
To try and climb this mountain all over again
When the fall from the peak was so sudden and
steep
When the humiliation felt so personal and deep
The scars from the fall seem like a tattoo instead
of a bruise

Every time I try something new, I know I will
inevitably lose.
I am the antidote to winning, the reverse of
progress
I am Mr Failure, the man who can never meet
success

He whispered in my ear and told me to see
That success and failure are a lens in how we
perceive
The night before a man knew success how
would he be deemed?
Redemption is for the fool who never stops
chasing what he once dreamed

Churchill said: 'Success is going from failure to
failure with the same enthusiasm'
You have only ever truly failed if you stop your
climb out the chasm
Otherwise keep climbing my son, for one day
you will see
That you were just a moment away from being
eternally free

True failure is never trying
So never stop failing, always keep smiling
True failure is never trying
So never stop failing, always keep smiling.

Mr Magic

I love rhyming
I love the way words flow easily
It seems to me
By making them rhyme somehow my troubles
inside appeases me
I can code my deepest feelings in secrecy
Hiding them in plain sight
While the people who read each line
Feel an ease from me

Sometimes I feel like I am wielding some
sorcery
Some magic, some arts which are meant for
wizardry
When I perform on stage
Each enchantment I make
Everyone is lost in my mystery

I can see their eyes say:
What words will come next?
Will it be a curse or a hex?
Will I feel joy or be vexed?
Will it end in sorrow or rest?

I can see their mind think:
Is he speaking about me?
Am I lost in my greed?
Can I also succeed?
Do I need to be free?

Each spell iii muster is His seed that will bear
fruit
His charm that will bewitch you to become a
new you
His prayer that intertwines in each rhyme
That one day we will feel anew, and float across
grace and time

This is the greatest magic trick one can truly
perform
That the conjurer is casting a spell to one day
self transform
The magician pledges they will turn and
disappear into the breeze
Reappearing and realising their soul is the true
prestige.

Mr Alone

When did you realise that in this world it's only
ever you and you?
Was it now?
Or have you known?
Or is it something that you yet believe to be
true?
I've always had a constant dialogue with myself,
apparently that's the first sign of being mad
Crazy right, that they shun you from speaking to
the one voice which will always understand

They said I was too mature as a child, a trouble
maker I was repeatedly called
All I did was ask questions about the creator,
who knew that would leave them appalled

I would always point out ideas and
contradictions and that would irk people's view
on their set beliefs
I thought life was about seeking truth, I didn't
realise how alone I must be
People only wanted to bow to the knowledge of
their priests

I've always known that I was always alone,
sometimes it's a lonely place to be
I've felt lonely with my closest friends and my
loving family
I've felt lonely in the loudest crowds and with
interesting company
I've felt lonely with the love of my life, even she
couldn't comfort me

When you know you are always alone, it's easy
to become a recluse
Feeling deserted, isolated and that no one will
ever be able to know you
I've been in that dark room, secluded and
separated from everything and everyone
In my remote island, where the dense and lonely
trees block out the collective sun

                    He looked at me with relief
                    He said finally you know the truth

But how you view being alone is completely up
to you
Yes you are alone
But being lonely means you haven't searched
hard enough
Keep digging
You will realise that you alone contain universal
love

Loving being alone is powerful
Loving being alone means you are in great
company
Keep talking to your inner voice which is
supernatural
Through that conversation, you alone will guide
yourself to being free.

Mr Busy

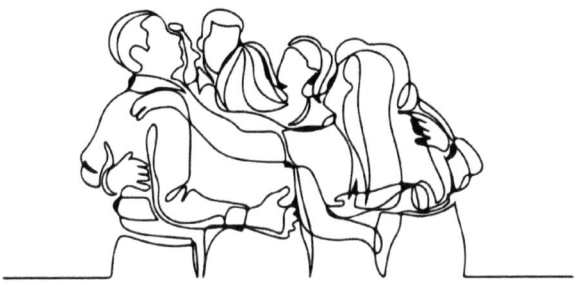

Busy is me but I still find the time to be free…
I am the man with a plan for every occasion
I even have a plan for when plans don't come to
fruition
But I'll drop them all if you want to come and
see me

No space in my calendar, not for nothing
Not even got time to tend to my needs
But if you are about and want to do something
I can squeeze you in between my sleep

So many things are happening where I need to
be present
But my mind is stuck reminiscing about the
events that have went
Boasting to someone about what excitement is
ahead

Can't be present in the present, the past and
future are on loop in my head.

Countries and cities need to be visited
Staying at home needs to be limited
I need a motive for every night
What else is there to do in this life?

He said we are so busy doing nothing we forget
what's the purpose of being alive
The purpose of life is to make your inner life the
purpose, instead of buzzing around outside,
caught in a beehive
The irony is that you have to taste every flower
to know the honey is sweetest in the garden that
lives beyond your bones
A pilgrim said only by leaving your house, will
you learn how to come back to your own home.

Only by leaving your house will you learn how
to return to your home.

Mr Procrastinator

Distractions, please come and distract me please
I invite you in to release me from my activities
Temptations please come and tempt me please
Take me away from my way and give me short
term relief
Burned by the anxiety of wanting to achieve
Goals taking too long to become my reality
I just need a few moments away from my dream
Just some time to sit back and breath
So that I can be distracted

Inattentive

      Diverted

Sidetracked

      Deflected

Away from what I promised me
Why does everything that shines looks like gold
to me?
I have no hold on my attention it's owned by
algorithm creators
And I've become another Mr Procrastinator

He put His hand on my head and grace filled my
entire being
He gazed into my eyes and showed me a whole
new way of seeing
He asked 'Are you working for you, or are you
serving me?'
In that moment, the need to succeed,
iii left at His pious feet

Because when work becomes His service,
Your life becomes His purpose
Distractions become distracted in trying to
distract your gaze
Temptations aren't tempted to try and tempt you
away
Only focus and love remain
All our procrastinations become delayed.

Mr iii

iii

Allow me to reintroduce myself. My name is…
Well it depends

Am I in a classroom?
Or on a stage?
Or surrounded by certain friends?

I could be Kish,
Mr Shah
Or the great Spoken Thiiird
My ego lives in all three
I know it, but I can't get rid of it, how absurd.

You can see my ego's shadow in every word
you've heard
It seeps through everything that I claim to be iii
Kishan is the primary identity that underlines
The split in my mind
Between teaching parallel straight lines and
People studying what I write in between them
A mathematician and an artist, half of me see its
reason
Easy to define logic but emotions are harder to
express

Probably because Spoken Thiiird is always
trying to impress
Too worried about what quirks other people's
interest
They always see less
But their opinions determine whether I'm a
success
An artist relies on word of mouth, mine and
theirs
That's why I'm so careful with these words
I treat each letter like they are the most precious
currency
Numbers add up in my bank from my creativity
which flows through me involuntarily.

I love sharing it with the ones that shape the
future of the Thiiird rock from the sun

When they say 'Mr Shah' it makes me laugh but
teaching is when I have the most fun
Endless joy to see the next Gen grow from their
x, y and zee
I teach them Maths but one day they'll thank me
for their history
I pray their future is filled with exponential
growth
It's the unspoken oath
For theirs and my success, I want them both
Only a goat can create a flock of goats

Yes I want to be the best of all time
That's why I write down every single one of my
rhymes

Spoken Thiiird to be on billboard signs

Because who am iii?
I am three people all of them combined

Kishan Shah, the human who lives
Mr Shah, the teacher who gives
Spoken Thiiird, the artist who persists

He sees me with all my identities as He inspired
the three iii's in my chosen name

He sees that iii put God as first and Him as
second, the ones to who iii bow down to and
pray
He sees that my grandparents are gold, my
parents silver and how much joy iii get from
bronze fame
He sees that the last Eye represents the pure one,
for which iii will see things as they are.
He sees that one day, Kishan, Spoken Thiiird
and Mr Shah will be His Superstar.

Chapter 3 - Colourful Hearts

Red passion

My blood boils so much, it comes out of my
eyes
Ironic, because sometimes I am calm when I
have red eye
Either I am in rage or I am stuck in my haze
Either way the red in my gaze is a warning sign
Two ways to show people, I am not aligned
Both are just phases of my two opposing planes
Being vexed and my remedy to alleviate the pain
Underneath it all my red cheeks will show
I'm shy to admit that I want a love so tight it
doesn't let go

I would bleed for my lover, my heart would
swell exponentially
Red roses and poems would be gifted endlessly
The ecstasy of a spiritual embrace
When heartbeats can be felt across both time and
space
A love so universal it touches the stars
Where we could feel close even though I could
be living on Mars
The red planet wouldn't be an obstacle for the
purest love
I have only experienced this with the one who
has reached the above

His love turned my red rage to soften and let go
No more red eye when you are addicted to His
glow
Just the redness of my heart always in His flow
Where I bleed His name and become one with
His Soul.

fifty shades of Brown

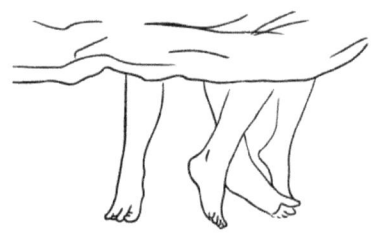

I've never written about sex before
That's kept under the covers
Behind closed doors
In a room that is dark
It's a whisper that needs to be explored

We don't speak about it, as our lips are saved
We also get tongue tied when trying to explain
Given a kiss of death to the conversation of how
life is made
Feel embarrassed to speak about something that
we feel will leave a stain

Girls' ears must stay virgins even though the
cats been out the bag
Instead they must read tall tales and enjoy its
climax

Only say God's name aloud when on
missionaries
The only downward dog they know is yoga
poses in the monastery

Turn a blind eye to our sons as the naked truth
can be blinding
Want his head in his blue books, that's his only
way of grinding
Want them to be articulate, attractive and their
backs to stand erect
Be chivalrous, if the girl wants a rain check he
must inspect if it is wet

Honestly
It always baffles me,
Why we've hidden sex so much in our brown
community
We are horny for gossip
Love the sound of our own moaning
Stay abreast with new scandals
Turned on for lies exposing

We leave the next generation to uncover it by
themselves and their chosen others
Rubbing out a chance of a safe future, just
endless heartbreaks and broken lovers

He said sex is physical
He said sex is necessary
He said sex is natural
He said sex is momentary

Sex should be spoken about, the whole picture
should come to light
It has become the world's worst held secret, but
we only try and hide
Because our lust for sex feels wrong, and if that
is right
Then the lust needs to go and the sex is left
behind.

Purple hearts

You were never in my universe
Then you became my whole universe
Then one day you left and my universe changed
Even though your light went away my universe
was never the same

Star struck lovers living on cloud number nine
A match made in heaven our destinies
intertwined
She felt like a divine find
I thanked the Gods for having her to share my
mind

Discovering parts of me I never knew existed
Magnetically attracted to the parts we resisted
Orbiting around each other's every need
Both of us gravitating towards a shared dream

Until the storm came, and lightening brought pain
Dark clouds gathered, bringing the illusion of night
I saw the darkness as a phase, keeping faith in the connection that we made
She however succumbed to the fright, calling dawn on our love life

Now I'm spiralling into oblivion, nothing to hold on to
My mind entering delirium, my future was only you
My night sky is filled with the past, the light gets fainter and further away
Now the cold rock of the moon fills my heart, a lunar eclipse that will last forever and a day

You were never in my universe
Then you became my whole universe
Then one day you left and my universe changed
Even though your light went away my universe was never the same

He tended to me seeing that my heart was scattered
Broken to pieces, bruised purple and blue

He gave me the space to figure out what
mattered
iii picked up my own pieces and had to give
them to You

He saw that iii had figured out that the winds of
time are testing
People come in seasons, all lovers cannot stay
And that in my life He was the greatest blessing
He was my rhyme and reason, as His light will
never fade away

His universe was the only one that promised
eternal life
His universe was the only one where iii could
feel everlasting light
His universe was a place that had to be realised
His universe was a space which could only be
seen through my Thiiird eye.

Dark love

Anakin Skywalker intrigues me
Had the light within but chose a path of darkness
What was it about the shadows mystique that he
Lost his lover which made him heartless?

Can suffering and pain, rewire our brain so we
fall in love with pain and suffering?
Can dark clouds and endless rain, normalise our
days, so light only comes when it's thundering?
If we have no hope of sunshine, we could easily
fall in love with blackness
If we don't feel we have a lifeline, it must be
easy to lose ourselves in madness

I have been there,
No hope, only despair
Turns to living without a care
For my own health and welfare

I start loving the pity I feel inside
Chipped shoulders become a point of pride
Having a circle so large it's comfortable to hide
Want the truth to hurt so never need to have lied

I have seen Anakin's path and I once took a step
There is a strange malicious fascination to what
lies ahead
A world where you do what's best for you and
only you
Narcissus warned us about drowning in your
own view

He asked me a few questions about this version
of love

Is it really love if it's full of control?
Is it really love if it comes from a place of lack?
Is it really love if you can't let go?
Is it really love if it is 'tit for tat'?

Falling in love with the darkness inside
Means your back will only feel the heat of the
light

Remember you are beyond any happenings to
you
Love is freedom, love is easy, love is truth

Kill your inner narcissus which dooms your
liberation
Become like the flower narcissi which blooms
with inspiration.

Pale apathy

I used to sleep walk when I was younger

Now my life feels like I'm stuck in a
slumber

The endless loop of getting through the day
The endless loop of getting through the day
The endless loop of getting through the day

And when it is finally night

Even sleep slips

Away

Praying for shade in the summer

Crying for sun in the cold

Hate that leaves fall in October

The days of new spring remind me that I'm
growing old

In death there will be peace

At least in the grave there is no room for fear

I can let my head rest in ease

Knowing I left all my hope over here

What kind of life is this

When failing seems easier than trying

When living feels harder than dying

He said:
'The tragedy of life is not death, the tragedy of
life is in allowing something to die within you
when you're living'

Life is Art,
Life is Logic
Life is Giving

Life is Fire
Life is Ice
Life is Burning

Life is Love
Life is Loss
Life is Learning

Life is Silence
Life is Loud
Life is Creating

Life is New
Life is Old
Life is Everlasting

Life is Enriching
Life is Enchanting
Life is Effervescent

Life is the greatest anti-depressant
Life is the greatest anti-depressant
Life is the greatest anti-depressant

Go out and live, don't just merely exist
Let your inner child break free from what your
adult mind resits
Let your apathy be the one to die

See life through your immaculate

eye,
eye, eye.

deep Blue sea

Shipwrecked, lost at sea
An infinite ocean underneath my feet
Furiously treading water, fighting against each
wave
In the depths of despair, the blue bed will be my
grave

How can this precious element that gives life, be
about to take mine
Drowning in my thoughts of sorrow, the irony
isn't hard to find
I didn't guard against my life, no one taught me
how to stay afloat
Now all there is is sadness, no rope or hope or
antidote

Does it matter how I got here?
All that matters is that I see fear
In every direction I cast my eyes,
Dear God my last moments will be the longest
baptise

I am lost in hopelessness in my own depression
Immersed in every emotion that suppresses my
expression
Yet when people see me, they meet a man who
looks calm and cool
They can't see that I am suffocating in me, lost
in my mental whirlpool
For the first time I prayed for a saviour and let
go of what I knew
Let go of any hope of trying to be the one that
can free me
So tired of myself and the mistakes I put myself
through
I stopped fighting against the water and fell to
my knees

His hand came from the air and took me from
the deep to sky blue.
He said all this time He had been waiting for my
prayers to be true
Waiting for me to realise that if iii truly wanted
to be able to swim with the tides

iii had to learn how to close my mind and open
my eyes
To the possibility that submitting to His will was
true wisdom
That submission to the God of Poseidon was
actually freedom
That iii was drowning in my thoughts which
could actually save my life
He showed me how to take one sip at a time
Instead of drinking everything which was
leading to my doom
He showed me to look for Him in the reflection
of the drops iii consume
So now iii only drink the water which is filtered
and pure
His shower of grace turned out to be my cure

White grief

The pain is silencing,
No words to write
My mind can't think
My pen no longer rhymes

She left too early
Her baby just arrived
Why did this happen?
I can't think of one reason why

She was an angel
The best of us
A warrior
The glue to the rest of us

My sister
We were bound by fate
A wife to another

Her true love, soulmate

What's he going through
How will he cope
Paralysed by grief
No sight of hope

Her mother, father and brother
How will they move
It happened so sudden
So much to loose

Her child will never know
The smile of her mum
The love that beholds
Outshines the light of the sun

Now darkness appears
The absence of her sight
So this is what true darkness must be
The absence of her light

His revolution in me, isn't that iii don't suffer,
it's that in spite of my suffering, iii still choose
to pass on love

My duty to Him is to ensure that iii can be
counted upon, to rise above feelings and to
perform my Dharma to the people that need me.

Through His teachings iii have developed
reasonable faith in knowing her spirit, essence,
soul, aatma, has moved to another form, and due
to her magnificence, she shed the karma that was
holding her back, gained karma that will move
her upwards and onwards, to eventually reaching
a state, where if iii reach, we will meet again.

He lets me miss her
He lets me mourn
But He shows me
The art of moving on.

Transparent tears

I used to cry when I was young
I was scared to go to school because I didn't
want to leave home
Cried out of anger and frustration when no one
listened to me
Cried when they used to hit me when I was
being naughty
From the ones who said they would always love
me
I cried when I was scared
I was scared all the time
Scared of the darkness of the night
The fear of what was on the other side
Cried when I was embarrassed
Cried when I let my family down

Cried tears when all I could give them was
frowns

I stopped crying when I was older
Didn't let my weakness take over me
It wasn't for me
I had control of me
I used to feel a lot
But I made sure the tears stayed inside
Better to suppress my eyes even if that means
the tears would leave me blind
I can't show frailty, fragility, delicacy
This is not my path
Had to ensure I wrapped stone around my heart
Emotionless, cold, don't even try look me in the
eye
All you'll get back is fear, as that is what is
trapped inside

And one fine day, something happened out of
surprise
iii saw God, and tears streamed down my eyes
This was the first time, when crying felt like
bliss
This was the first time, iii was truly crying from
happiness
And the heart made of stone, starting melting
away
My tears told me, this God was here to stay

My tears told me, tell your fear goodbye
Now only joy will pour out of all three of your
eyes.

Green grass

When I look at my garden I see the weeds before
I see the trees
The parts that are uneven, the parts with the
withered leaves
I see the fruit which is unripened, the stones
which are unturned
The bushes which need trimming, the soil which
has been sunburned

When I look at their garden, everything seems
proper and prim
Every twig seems right, every blade of grass
seems to have been carefully trim
Even the parts that are slightly bent seem to give
it an artistic flair

My garden will never be as magical, no matter
how much I care

He said that my comparison is the thief of my
joy
That chasing perfection is the quickest way for
me to destroy
My self-worth and love and to be grateful for all
that iii am
iii have luscious grass, how could fruit grow in
barren sand?

Be inspired by others, never try and imitate
Let them be them and let you be you
Let envy turn to generosity and let your garden
illuminate
Who you are and what you choose

The grass is the greenest where it has the most
attention
Attend to your own and you'll love every
imperfection.

Purposeful Endings

Three steps ahead

I'm hesitant

To show you a secret of mine
That will no longer be mine
Once left from my mind
Onto the page that I write
As when the ink dries
The scribe left behind
Is sealed in eternal time
Which will no longer be mine

That's why I'm
Scared

To share with you a view so private
I've had to store it and hide it
In the remotest island
Even radar cannot find it

I've even fortified it
Classified it
Solidified it

As some things are best left unsaid
Until the time is correct
When we get closer to death
We hear truth best
And I dread
That what I have written is released and read
Before I am not yet dead

You see
My demise is the only thing I know will be
So I remain three steps ahead before time comes
for me
I began preparing my secret as soon as He
Awakened me from my dream
A slumber I was in so deep
That I never believed
Death truly comes for me
Or anyone in my proximity
He planted the seed
For me to plan a w.a.y.e to consciously leave
As best as can be
To close chapters on tales that no longer fit my
story
This is what He taught me

It starts with The Art of Living
Which bleeds into the Art of Loving
Expands in the Art of Laughing
Ends in the Art of Leaving

One day I will leave
And my secret will be unleashed
As then it will be time to remove its seal
And its contents will be a testament that reveals

My close friendship to a dark cloud which
terrifies
Yet only the blessed see it's lining is made of
silver light
It's been said you have actually been given three
lives
The second one begins when you realise
There is only this one lifetime
To open up the Thiiird Eye
Which shows how you can never die

This secret of mine

Will be shared at a time

That this version

Finally

Says

'Good B(eye).'

The Message

If I left this Earth tonight
What would be the last words that I write?
What would be the feeling I want to convey?
If tonight would be the night I never get to see a
new day
What would I say?
What would I want people to know?
I would speak entirely about a Soul that has met
His Soul

I would urge everyone to find the One who lives
in light
And not to stop until they have found 'The One'
They'll know when they have got it right when
His shine is brighter than any sun
Even if it takes them their whole life to find the
One who is complete in every single way

And even if they don't find the One in this life,
they would not have wasted a single day

They wouldn't have wasted a single breath if
they lived in pursuit of finding their guide
Who knows the route that leads to them, that
leads to truth, through the avenue that leads
inside
If they live a life without such a search no matter
what they go onto achieve
They would have never awoken to the true
reality
They'll be a rich man whose wealth is inside a
dream

And if they are so blessed to meet such a master
then they will have to do the hardest thing
To lay their crown onto Their One's feet for they
are a mere pauper compared to a true King
If they can do this with sincerity, they're on the
path to be eternally free, as they'll follow every
order with no mind of their own
And with His Grace over your head, He'll move
all obstacles till it's just you and your Soul

Because in this life what else is there to do than
to find out who we truly are?
What if I told you that you hold more light in
you than than all the combined stars?

I know we do because I have met a Soul who
has touched Their Soul
This is what I would say to you, this is what I
would want to be known

If tonight would be the night that I never got to
see a new day
This would be the last feeling that I would want
to truly convey
These would be the last words that I would ever
want to write
If I left this Earth tonight, I will tell you:

Get out of your Darkness and find Your Guide
They'll be the One made of only Light

His Light In My Darkness

What is the worst thing that can happen to you?
Think death, think grief, think about the blackest
view
Envision the saddest truth
Imagine endless pain without even a chance of
rescue
What if I said to you this was on a permanent
loop

The same feeling again and again and again and
again
It forms and then ends and then forms and then
ends
If it comes again, is it really the end?
Or just the start, the beginning, the arrival of
more regret?

Just endless suffering, shattering every part of
one's heart
Which becomes blackened and bruised and
ultimately falls apart
Tormented by this world, beating through the
stains of past scars
Stuck in an infinite cycle, in the East we call this
Sansar

This is the predicament we are all in,
Looking for joy in a place where it has never
lived
Searching every day to find happiness over
there.
Do we not become weary in running here, there
and everywhere?

Searching for the end of the rainbow, we can
never realise
That every colour we seek has always been
inside

Searching for the end of the rainbow, we can
never realise
That every colour we seek has always been
inside

Until

Arrives

The Guide

Darkness is not inherent, it's the absence of light
To defeat blindness, all we need is true sight
The role of the Highest Soul is to show the route
inside
To end the cycle, to bring dawn from the night

That's what He did for me
He saved my soul, He set me free
He showed me truth
He showed me bliss
He paved my route to true happiness

He gave me life, He gave me joy
He made me a man from a struggling boy
He basked me with grace
He showed me an escape
From my flaws and all of my dark negatives
He shined His light on me
He shined His light on me

That is why He is the ink within my words
That is why He is the one that is above Spoken
Thiiird

He is my Guide, He is my Guru, He is God to
me
As He was the One that showed me Gods in me
As He was the One that showed me Gods in me

He is my heart for without iii would be heartless
He is the light in my darkness
He is the light in my darkness.

Milton Keynes UK
Ingram Content Group UK Ltd.
UKHW050625140724
445574UK00027B/701